Cancel Culture

The Pitfalls of the Woke Ideology

BROOKS

Copyright© 2024

by

Dr. Steven Brooks

Published by Professional Employee Training Services LLC

All Rights Reserved.

ISBN: 9798880091140

DEDICATION

To Everyone Who Learned from the Past and Changed the Future!

FROM THE AUTHOR

Words of truth based upon experiences become reminders of what has and has not succeeded. Canceling anything historical is erasing the opportunity to change the future positively. The blind cannot lead the blind on a tightrope – from the mind of author Dr. Steven Brooks.

Here are some words I consider essential in life and in this book.

"These men turn from the right way to walk down dark paths. They take pleasure in doing wrong, and they enjoy the twisted ways of evil."

"But these oppressors know nothing; they are so ignorant! They wander about in darkness while the entire world is shaken to the core."

It's fairly easy to send an innocent person to prison. It's very difficult to get one out. – Author John Grisham

An Overview and Consideration

The counterintuitive nature of erasing historic events per *"woke philosophy"* is beyond ignorance. The concept of *"wokeness"* has gained traction as a movement advocating social justice, equality, and inclusivity. However, while its intentions seem noble, the methodologies stunt cultural growth, change, and diversity. The divisive nature of cancel culture is the perfect tool to segregate America, which insults the lives, philosophies, and sacrifices of civil rights leaders like Martin Luther King. Initially, cancel culture was a fledgling idea that became a prominent battle cry fueled by anger and negativity toward anyone who questioned the motives.

The hostility from cancel culture supporters created an immediate division spurred by biased liberal news agencies who failed to share the totality of circumstances. This skewed perspective accelerated contempt between supporters and challengers. Political parties immediately formed alliances with one side or the other, which perpetuated debate and additional division.

The American society that once held the core values that every person was created equal fell by the wayside, and bullies arose demanding preferential treatment because of race, gender, sexual orientation, and anything else that could be thrown into the mix. , which sparked intense debates and defined the ideological lines within communities.

Proponents argue that cancel culture holds individuals and institutions accountable for their actions. What actions? The actions defined by anyone who "feels" they were not identified or treated fairly. In other words, anything they perceived – emotionally biased perspectives - that goes against the cancel culture mantra. This mentality of "it's our way or the highway" spotlights cancel culture supporters as tyrants and bullies who are cry babies whining about not getting everything handed to them. Look at the perspectives and ideals cancel culture supporters want you to abide by as you forfeit your perspectives and ideals. Am I the only one who sees a hypocritical double-speak and double-standard? What have proponents of cancel culture failed to consider? Division, intolerance, and social fragmentation, to name a few. Indeed, the phenomenon of cancel culture has and continues to contribute to the growing polarization and segregation within America.

This research proves the multifaceted damning nature of cancel culture by examining its origins, mechanisms, impacts, and implications for society.

By synthesizing diverse perspectives using empirical evidence, we discover the need for a balanced sociological approach that acknowledges the legitimate concerns of "wokeness" while fostering constructive dialogue that encourages reconciliation. Work together!

Considerations

In legal and contractual contexts, consideration refers to exchanging something of value between parties as part of an agreement. It is a fundamental element, demonstrating that each party is giving up something of value or assuming a legal obligation in exchange for what the other party provides.

Consideration can take various forms, including money, goods, services, promises, or refraining from specific actions. Essentially, it represents the bargained-for exchange that forms the basis of a contract, indicating that both parties have willingly agreed with mutual understanding and intention. Moreover, consideration ensures that contracts are not merely gratuitous promises but enforceable commitments backed by legal validity. We can only succeed by listening, considering, and promoting unity.

Consideration 1 - Bias

Cancel culture thrives within echo chambers, where like-minded individuals reinforce each other's beliefs and perspectives. Social media platforms, in particular, have facilitated the formation of ideological bubbles where dissenting voices are silenced or ostracized. As a result, individuals are less exposed to diverse viewpoints and less inclined to engage in constructive dialogue with those who hold different opinions, leading to heightened tribalism and polarization.

Consideration 2 - Fear

The fear of being "*canceled*" stifles open discourse and fosters self-censorship. In such an environment, individuals may hesitate to express dissenting or controversial views for fear of public backlash, social ostracization, or even professional repercussions. This climate of fear undermines the principles of Constitutional free speech and intellectual perspectives while hampering the free exchange of ideas – debates - necessary for a healthy democratic society.

Discussion and dialogue provide the opportunity for enlightenment and understanding.

Consideration 3 - Us vs. Them Mentality

Cancel culture often operates within an "us vs. them" framework where individuals are categorized as allies or adversaries based on their belief in particular ideological norms. This binary worldview oversimplifies complex issues and promotes a mentality of moral absolutism, where individuals are judged solely upon their perceived ideological choices rather than the content of their character or the context of their actions. Such tribalistic thinking erodes empathy and understanding, further deepening societal divisions and promoting intolerance and anger.

Pointing fingers at each other fuels disagreement and division, not understanding.

Consideration 4 - Selective Outrage and Double Standards

Critics of cancel culture often highlight its tendency to apply inconsistent accountability standards. While specific individuals or groups may face swift and severe consequences for perceived transgressions, others may receive leniency or acclaim for similar behavior. This selective outrage undermines the credibility of cancel culture as a force for justice and fuels resentment and distrust among different segments of society – aka, division.

Some people see one criminal, as others see another criminal. We cannot hope for change. Change takes place through positive interaction and dialogue.

Consideration 5 - Erosion of Social Trust

Cancel culture undermines social trust by fostering an environment of suspicion and antagonism. When individuals fear they are targeted for expressing dissenting views or engaging in unpopular behavior, they are less likely to trust others and more inclined to withdraw into homogeneous social circles where they feel safe from scrutiny. This erosion of social trust weakens the bonds of unity that hold diverse communities together and impedes efforts to bridge cultural, ideological, and socioeconomic divides.

Division never promotes unity!

Consideration 6 - The Importance of History

History is the backbone of cultural identity, providing a narrative thread connecting past, present, and future generations. By erasing or sanitizing historical events, we risk severing this vital link and depriving ourselves of history's lessons and insights. Understanding where we came from is essential for charting a path forward and fostering cultural growth and change by knowing what mistakes to avoid.

Learn from the past, and live for the future.

Consideration 7 - Embracing Complexity

Cultural growth and change are inherently complex processes that require grappling with diverse perspectives, ideologies, and experiences. Erasing historic events simplifies this complexity, creating a sanitized version of history that fails to reflect the diverse tapestry of human existence. Actual cultural growth comes from engaging with the full spectrum of our shared history, even its uncomfortable and challenging aspects.

Everything must be considered and examined carefully.

Consideration 8 - Preserving Diversity

Diversity thrives on the richness of human experiences, including those that are painful or controversial. By erasing historical events, we risk homogenizing cultural narratives and stifling the diversity of voices and perspectives contributing to our collective understanding of the world. Embracing the complexities of history is essential for preserving cultural diversity and fostering inclusivity within society.

There will always be differences in opinions and perspectives, which contributes to diversity and understanding while removing division.

Consideration 9 - Learning from the Past

Historical events, even those that are difficult to confront, offer invaluable opportunities for learning and growth. They provide insights into the successes and failures of past generations, illuminating pathways for progress and transformation in the present and future. Erasing historic events denies us the chance to learn from past mistakes and undermines our ability to navigate the complexities of the world around us.

Learning from the past cannot be accomplished by erasing history. History must be examined and embraced.

Consideration 10 - Fostering Dialogue and Understanding

Cultural growth and change are facilitated by open dialogue and exchange of ideas. Erasing historic events stifles this dialogue, creating echo chambers where dissenting voices are silenced and alternative perspectives are marginalized. Actual cultural growth requires embracing diversity of thought and engaging in constructive conversations about our shared history and the values that shape our society.

Talk isn't cheap when it contributes to understanding.

Consideration 11 - The Balanced Approach

In advocating for social justice and equality, it is essential to balance acknowledging past injustices and fostering a forward-looking vision for the future. While confronting the legacies of oppression and discrimination is crucial, so is preserving our cultural heritage's richness and diversity. A balanced approach to cultural growth and change embraces the complexities of historical good and evil while remaining open to new ideas and perspectives.

Nobody wins when the scales are not balanced!

Consideration 12 - The Illusion of Progress

Woke philosophy often promotes removing or suppressing historic events deemed offensive or insensitive by contemporary standards. However, this approach ignores the fundamental truth that progress is not achieved by erasing the past but by confronting it head-on and learning. Change requires acknowledging the complexities of history, even its darkest, and learning to build a more just and equitable future.

Erasing the past does not preserve the future!

Consideration 13 - Cultural Amnesia

In the rush to sanitize history, woke ideology risks fostering collective amnesia—a willful forgetting of the events and experiences that have shaped our societies. This erasure deprives us of valuable lessons and undermines cultural diversity and richness. We risk homogenizing our cultural landscape and stifling the vibrant tapestry of experience by suppressing dissenting voices and uncomfortable truths.

Just because you don't want to remember it doesn't mean it never happened.

Consideration 14 - Embracing Complexity

Cultural growth and change are inherently complex processes that require grappling with diverse perspectives, ideologies, and experiences. Erasing historic events simplifies this complexity, creating a sanitized version of history that fails to reflect the diverse tapestry of human existence. Cultural growth comes from engaging with the full spectrum of our shared history, even when it's uncomfortable, complex, and challenging.

Difficult and complex issues do not stop you from learning!

Consideration 15 - Preserving Diversity

Diversity thrives on the richness of human experiences, including those that are painful or controversial. By erasing historical events, we risk homogenizing cultural narratives and stifling the diversity of voices and perspectives contributing to our collective understanding of the world. Embracing the complexities of history is essential for preserving cultural diversity and fostering inclusivity within society.

Diversity begins at home and in the neighborhood.

Consideration 16 - The Tyranny of Revisionism

At its core, woke philosophy champions the revisionist approach to history, which judges past events through the lens of present-day morality. This tendency to apply modern sensibilities to historical contexts distorts the truth and undermines the complexity of human experience. By erasing or sanitizing uncomfortable truths, we risk perpetuating a sanitized version of history that fails to reflect the full spectrum of human triumphs and tribulations.

Saying it never happened does not change history; it changes the truth!

Consideration 17 - Erasing the Uncomfortable

In pursuing social justice, the woke movement often seeks to erase events or figures deemed morally reprehensible by contemporary standards. Whether it be removing statues, renaming buildings, or banning books, these acts of erasure not only sanitize history but also deprive future generations of the opportunity to confront uncomfortable truths and learn from past mistakes.

Just because one person's belief does not align with your perspectives and makes you uncomfortable does not give you the right to remove it.

Consideration 18 - Losing Context and Perspective

History is a complex tapestry woven from the threads of time, culture, and circumstance. Each event exists within its historical context, shaped by its era's prevailing ideologies, norms, and values. By imposing modern standards onto the past, we risk oversimplifying historical narratives and losing sight of the nuanced factors that contributed to the events.

Without the proper perspective and necessary resources, you can't see something directly before you!

Consideration 19 - The Illusion of Moral Superiority

In the quest to cleanse history of its perceived sins, the woke movement often adopts an air of moral superiority, casting judgment upon figures of the past without acknowledging the complexities of their lives and legacies. This self-righteous attitude stifles meaningful dialogue and breeds resentment and division within society as differing interpretations of history clash in the public sphere.

Never consider yourself to be better than anyone. The exterior of a person does not reveal their true identity. Humble people stand tall before the proud. Seek to understand others, not attack them.

Consideration 20 - The Threat to Academic Freedom

At the heart of any vibrant democracy lies the principle of academic freedom—the unfettered pursuit of knowledge and truth, unbound by ideological constraints or censorship. However, the rise of woke ideology has increasingly encroached upon this fundamental principle, stifling dissenting viewpoints and enforcing a monolithic interpretation of history that brooks no opposition.

The closing of minds will eventually close schools. When that happens, nobody learns.

Consideration 21 - Embracing Complexity and Preserving History

In the face of these challenges, we must reclaim the true essence of history—one that embraces complexity, diversity, and nuance. Rather than seeking to erase or sanitize the past, we must confront its uncomfortable truths head-on, acknowledging the full spectrum of human experience and learning from the mistakes of our predecessors.

When history is remembered, it should never be replayed as an image of something terrible but as an opportunity to create something extraordinary from it!

Consideration 22 - A Call to Vigilance

As guardians of history, we are tasked with a solemn duty—to preserve the integrity of the past and protect it from the perils of ideological censorship. Through education, dialogue, and critical thinking, we can foster a more nuanced understanding of events that celebrate triumphs and grapple with their complexities equally.

We must protect the past to preserve the future. Hindsight provides foresight!

Consideration 23 - Echoes of Time

In the corridors of history, whispers of bygone eras linger, resonating through the annals of time. Whether triumphant or tragic, each event contributes to the intricate tapestry of human existence. Like threads in a grand tapestry, these events intertwine to shape the collective identity of societies worldwide. However, in pursuing progress and the quest for a brighter future, a dangerous temptation exists to erase specific considerations from this narrative.

As we mentally walk in the wake of our past, we realize the impact of how each event sculpted our minds and the character of every person.

Consideration 24 - The Fabric of Memory

At the heart of any civilization lies its memory—a repository of shared experiences, lessons learned, and stories passed down through generations. History is the cornerstone of this collective memory, providing a roadmap of where we have been and guiding us toward our aspirations. To tamper with this delicate fabric is to risk unraveling the very essence of society itself.

As you stand and look into history, you get to look within yourself.

Consideration 25 - Lessons Forgotten

In the past pages lie invaluable lessons waiting to be unearthed. From the rise and fall of empires to the struggles for liberation and equality, each consideration offers insights into the human condition and the complexities of our world. Removing these lessons from the narrative denies us the opportunity to learn from past mistakes and grow as a society.

Sometimes, you may forget things that require you to return to the past to bring that memory to the present.

Consideration 26 - Silencing Voices

History is not solely comprised of grand events and momentous occasions; it is also a painting created from the stories of individuals whose voices deserve to be heard. From marginalized communities to oppressed peoples, each voice adds depth and richness to the overarching narrative of humanity, understanding, and our culture. To erase these voices is to perpetuate injustice and silence the stories of those marginalized by the dominant discourse.

Closing the mouths of people also closes the minds of everyone.

Consideration 27 - Distorting Reality

The erasure of historical events is not merely an act of forgetting; it is a deliberate distortion of reality—a rewriting of the past to fit a particular narrative or agenda. By selectively omitting certain events or perspectives, we risk perpetuating falsehoods and denying future generations access to the truth. In doing so, we undermine the very foundation of democracy and sow the seeds of distrust within society.

Distorting the truth of reality distorts the truth of democracy and perpetuates lies that eventually become distorted truths.

Consideration 28 - Honoring the Past Will Embrace the Future

In the face of this looming threat, we must safeguard the integrity of history and preserve the legacy of those who came before us. By confronting the darker Considerations of our past and acknowledging the injustices committed, we pave the way for a more just and equitable future. Only by honoring the past can we hope to build a better tomorrow—one rooted in truth, justice, and reconciliation.

When the past, full of knowledge and experience, takes the present by the hand, they embrace each other and share their experiences.

Consideration 29 – Walk in the Footsteps of Giants

As we stand at the crossroads of the past and present, let us heed the lessons we have learned and forge a path toward a brighter future. We must embrace the complexities of our shared heritage and celebrate the diversity of human experience. And let us never forget that it is only by confronting the shadows of history that we can truly bask in the light of progress. Ultimately, it is not the erasure of history that defines us but rather our steadfast commitment to preserving history for generations to come.

If we carefully follow the steps of others, we will fill their shoes. In doing so, we will also see their missteps and chart a new course that safely leads others to success.

Epilogue

In a world marked by diversity and complexity, embracing the richness of individual differences and perspectives is essential for fostering harmony, understanding, and collective progress.

Rather than adhering to rigid expectations or predefined roles, we must cultivate environments where authenticity, acceptance, and collaboration flourish. By celebrating the unique qualities and experiences that each person brings to the table, we can harness the power of diversity to generate innovative solutions, bridge cultural divides, and build stronger communities.

Working together requires us to set aside preconceptions and biases, to listen with empathy, and to engage with humility and openness. Through genuine connection and mutual respect, we can transcend superficial labels and embrace the humanity that unites us all.

Let us recognize that our differences are not barriers but invitations to learn, grow, and love together, creating a world where everyone is valued, accepted, and empowered to contribute their authentic selves to the tapestry of human experience.

Thank you for letting me share these words with you. The time for our nation to grow positively is now! Not tomorrow or next week. Every day without unity widens the divide that separates us. Let us never cancel the culture; let us create our culture.

www.ingramcontent.com/pod-product-compliance
Lightning Source LLC
Chambersburg PA
CBHW060823260726
48660CB00003B/1072